GROWING
INTO THE BLUE

Other Books by Ulrich Schaffer
LOVE REACHES OUT
A GROWING LOVE
SEARCHING FOR YOU
FOR THE LOVE OF CHILDREN
SURPRISED BY LIGHT
GREATER THAN OUR HEARTS
WITH OPEN EYES

GROWING INTO THE BLUE

ULRICH SCHAFFER

with Photographs by the Author

1817

Harper & Row, Publishers, San Francisco

Cambridge, Hagerstown, New York, Philadelphia
London, Mexico City, São Paulo, Sydney

FIRST EDITION

LIBRARY OF CONGRESS CATALOGING IN PUBLICATION DATA

Schaffer, Ulrich, DATE
  Growing into the blue.

  I. Title.
PR9199.3.S26G65   1984   811'.54   83-48463
ISBN 0-06-067089-4

84 85 86 87 88 10 9 8 7 6 5 4 3 2 1

For Margie—

you stand for many of us

in your desire to grow
and the fear of the experience,

in the joy you find in moving on
and the pain of living in the new,

in your dream to be free
and in the weight of that freedom

Blue is reminiscent
of the water
in which my soul swam
when God created it
before he divided
the land and the sea.

I was his idea.

To this and all other ideas
he added a secret movement,
like a wind
    before there was air,
like a rise
    before there was up and down,
like an explosion
    before there was matter,

a movement,
so that nothing
ever needs to be the same
from second to second,
and he called that movement,
that green thrust,

growth.

The deeper the blue
to which I aspire,
the more luminescent
will be the light
that I still catch with my life.

God is in both:
the background
and the light.

God grows toward us
as we grow toward him.

Don't believe those without visions,
they live in perpetual winter.
They cannot see the green crown
in the bleak branches.
Their fear renders the world
in shades of gray.

Let your vision
color the world.

There are times
when we die into the blue.

The sky is not an opening.
Its blue mocks us.
We do not seem to grow.
Life shrivels.
We have no future.
Only the spot we stand on
remains a refuge.

It is then,
like the magic seed
in the fairy tale,
that we grow,
without knowing it.

He experiences growth
on the silvery background of death.
Colors receive their brilliance and movement
from the darkness they are overcoming.
He does not grow like a lark,
spiraling into spring air.

Winds drive through him.
Words cut his eyes.
Fires burn his feet.
Dead ends offer despair.
He is declared lost.
He is abandoned.

But in it all
he mostly stands.
He emerges on the life side,
not measuring his growth,
but taller.

A survivor
and therefore a challenger.

I will not be stifled
by those who deny growth,
by ideas which forbid unfolding,
by laws which suppress maturing.

I will not be intimidated
by the dictates of permanence.
I will not be smothered
by pretty mediocrity.
I will not be restrained
by the safe-players.

I will protest the denial of life
and forge ahead.
How else will you and I meet?
The common place will not feed us.
We will starve in the middle of plenty.

I will make contact with myself
and grow toward you
with that extra sense of touch.
I will see you with the inner eye,
hear your unspoken words,
walk more than a mile with you.

I will be unpredictable,
I will live.

Guard your vision jealously.
It is attainable.
Take your yearning seriously.
It is the presence of God in you.

Gather strength
when all growth is frozen
and then burst forth
to let your vision grow again.

Color it,
give it substance.
Paint yourself into its center
where you belong.

Be at home with yourself.
God is.

Green-thumbed God,
my ancient gardener,
I spread my branches
to treat you to shade
so we can talk.

My relationship to you
has been ambiguous.
I have always shivered
under your pruning knife,
but I have lapped up your watering.
I was hurt that you did not protect me
from the destructive winds,
but I trust your accurate eye
to design my future shape.
I rest in your dream of me.
I will reward your quiet murmurings
(encouraging me to grow)
by pushing up another shoot.

Before the cold of winter,
I will throw myself
into a magnificence
that will take your breath away.
I will be flowing gold,
transparent yellow,
I will be sun behind shifting sun
in every leaf.

Can you hear
that I talk to you through colors?
Are you listening
to the love prayers of my leaves?

Growth,
not toward the ultimate goal
at the expense of the present.

Growth,
not away from something
as a fearful recoiling.

Growth,
not as duty,
not as sign of success,
not as demonstration.

But as the natural act of expanding,
of filling the world with living,
with being
and being
and being.

I am.
Therefore I am always becoming.

. . . this almost secret drive
up through the humus
to layers of earthlight

. . . this silent but strong push
against all forms of permanent death
toward freedom

. . . this fragile upheaval
this everyday magic
this regular wonder

. . . this thrust to be recognized
by color and texture
by dream and vision

. . . a blade of grass . . .
. . . a grain of wheat . . .
. . . a giant sequoia in one seed . . .

it's in you
give in to it

The weight,
found in all hues of blue,
comes toward me.
I begin to weigh my own weight at first,
then a ton,
then the weight of the world.
I am too heavy and cannot lift off.
All prayers seem pale.
God is too bright
and too perfect.

I seem to shrink
and become impervious
to a speckled world.
I turn to stone,
but I know it is a stone in transition,
hurtling toward awareness.

I sink deeper and deeper into the blue.
Underworld caverns take me in
on my way through to the other side.
I know that there all weight
is converted into lightness.

Oh, how I will jump and fly
when I reach the other side;
and I will sink into the red,
yellow and green.
But I will always love blue the best
because it gave me weight
and taught this stone
to feel and bleed.

I see the air blue and beckoning,
I will rise into it
like a weightless balloon
and burst into life
full of splendor.

Will you rise with me
and match my wish with your energy
to be alive
through and through?
Will you draw me to the limit
and beyond,
where all growth
is into a God
much larger than yours
and mine?

I have decided for life.
I have decided to grow,
to do more than survive,
to grow through the fog to the sun,
that attractive star.

I have decided to ignore
the coaxings, the threats,
the requests to turn into stone.
I have chosen to keep in motion.

I have decided
to take my chances with the abyss,
to weather the painful in-betweens,
to wake in my own blood,
to mourn my lost innocence
in the process of growth,
because all growth has as its heartflower
pain in its endless variations,
and its petals
are the many colors of suffering.

But I have also decided
to overcome all obstacles,
to stand triumphant at the end,
the child turned into man
and into child again.

All growing is changing
from one state to another.
Leaving a world behind,
entering the fear of the unaccustomed:
of colors that don't blend,
of holy words that jar,
of fractures that give rise to visions.

We have left one realm
but have not arrived at the other.
We have given up one safety
but not gained another..
Above the gazing crowd
the trapeze artist lets go of his swing,
and then, if his timing is right,
seizes the other swing,
without asking time to stop for him.
That is the flight into growth.

That is the changeover
in which we experience our nakedness
to the point of hurting.
But there is not real growth without leaping,
without burning bridges
and standing wide-eyed and shivering
on a new shore.

And yet
without growth
there is nothing.

Wanting to know
with my mind and heart,
with my fingertip senses,
with the pit of my stomach,
with the skin of my whole being,

wanting to experience,
to live and relive,
to hold,
to let go,
to find,
to forget,

are all
in their mysterious way
expressions of my deep desire
to grow.

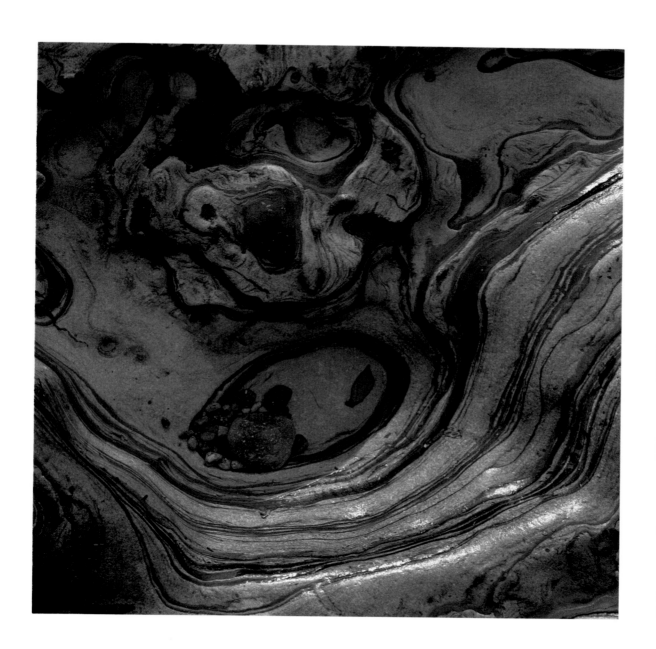

I take a walk on the beach.
The waves are my brothers.
Like mine, their bodies are temporary.
Their flying crests are a last upheaval.

The birds are my sisters.
Like mine, their flying time is limited.
But their flight is complete and perfect now.
Their heaven is here.

Sand is my life.
Fine and flowing
it runs out in certainty
and cannot be held.

I walk through my life.

God,
I have grown enough.
I want to abandon my ambitions,
at least for this day.
I am content to be
just one of the many,
the average,
the mediocre,
the mid-sized.

My mind
cannot take any more infusions of pain,
my body is too slow
to catch the light,
my eyes are clouded
from too many tears.
To believe that growing is crucial
is an act of self-denial
that I cannot perform today.

Today,
at least this one day,
this 14,575th day,
allow me to rest from my goals,
from your visions for me,
to just be
one of the millions
on an ordinary
tolerable path.

I am unfinished, a work in progress.

I touch my skin.
It is so new that at times
it does not know what it feels.
Learning is slow.
Decoding intonations,
separating similar hues,
interpreting movements,
recognizing patterns,
realizing the hidden rhythm,
all takes time.

I am slow, God,
but I won't ask for your patience
because you have determined
the speed of my growth.
I will accept myself
even when I am an impediment
to my own completion.

I accept your timing
with a measure of impatience,
but there is also comfort in slowness,
in that deliberate, determined snail's pace.

I follow my built-in compass.
I hone my instincts.
I reevaluate my guidance system.
I let go of ballast.
I test my wings.

I don't make bargains with half-measures.
I am on the road of learning.
I see the clarity of mirrors grow.
I spell my way to understanding.
I don't want an illustrious standstill.
I am perpetual motion.
Standing still is the motion of rest.

I have one goal: to touch the blue.
I want limitlessness as my ultimate skin.
I am not content with numbing repetition.
I want the cutting edge,
the lifted boundaries,
the forging vanguard,
the brazenness of life,
a cut of the unencumbered.

That is the profile
of which I have to remind myself.

As if dreaming himself
he dreams of God,
and God is the hewer of wood,
the drawer of water.
He is the gardener
with peas in his hand.
He is the wisdom in the sunflower.
He is the shoot infused with energy.
He is the central ring in the sequoia.
He is the kernel,
is the chlorophyll,
is

He is,
is going on,
turning and becoming his own dream,
growing into the blue of blues,
and with the help of dreamers
he completes the circle
and finally rests in his own rhythm.

It is such a distance
to that other shore,
but I believe it to be reachable
and dip my oars in again.
The day rolls through its colors,
from blue to black
to light and back to blue again.

When I open my eyes
I still have not arrived.
But this young day invites me
to float into its new chance.
The waves I travel
are creations of light.
Sometimes the blood
shining in their troughs
is mine.

I have done all this
thousands of times.
Each day has a tax and a prize.
Their sequence is a string of pearls,
a row of open knives.

I will not let go.
My hands close around the oars
in their determined cramp.
I will not let go.
I focus on the thin thread
between my hands on the oars
and the shore of light
that lives in me like a crystal mountain.

Some days are marked
by a fury of growth,
a freedom of expansion
that rejects all limits.

Then the air wishes to be filled
with bursting life,
so direct and consuming
that no one will dare
to intervene
because it is the time of life.

And then there are days
that seem to suffer
under a perverse power
that shrinks and shrivels
all attempts at life.

Then the ground is filled with stones
that leave roots wasted.
All rushes of energy
are futile gestures
and death looks on
without shame.
And again no one will dare
to intervene
in the powerful sweep of death.

And yet each day is necessary
to complete the intricate pattern,
to create the rhythm
in which the universe expands,
to feel that first breath
still reverberating in the molecule.

All growing
is leaping
past myself
to a form
that I have seen
in what I take
to be
His mirror.

That whole me,
that healed
I-am-I.
A luminous breath.

I enter the taproot,
the lateral roots,
the root hairs,
I flow through
the xylem and phloem tubes,
I course through the veins
in the multiple shapes of leaves,
like some gnome on a mission
to find secret recipes for growth.

And I find the secret everyone knows:
a pinch of persistence,
an eyeful of observation,
a measure of restlessness,
an abundance of yearning
and a sprinkling of vehemence.

I seek out the bluest spot
in a blue sky
and aim myself into it.
This is a day of growth.

I will live on air
and collect the sun's energy
to feed my resources,
to convert the black soil
into offerings of color.

No longer will I be a stepson
to the ecstatic grass,
held and swayed
by the fertile spring wind.

I will grow into that blue,
toward God,
where my seed was planted,
thus completing the circle.

Don't turn to stone,
continue to feel:
the gentleness of the wind,
the hardness of hail,
feel your faltering hands,
survive that strong yearning
like ice and fire.

Don't turn to stone.
Remain pervious to the fluid of life,
be tissue that can breathe
and gives itself to the sun.
Risk bursting
because you can't contain
the overripe fullness of life.

Don't turn to stone,
continue to walk,
don't grow roots.
Experience the air as a street
and take a chance along the abyss.

And even if you fall,
remember that falling
is the privilege of the living.

Only the stature is left,
the shape of things that were.
The crown of the valley,
the overview, the age.

But it has stopped growing.
It will rot on the inside
and some wind will take
what the fire left.

What was once grandeur
is now exposed surface
and fair game
to hostile elements.

Past growth
is a vague memory.

When God draws only faint lines around me,
when the horizon is a mere suggestion,
when my thoughts are light enough to fly,
when gentleness is an aura on all things,
I grow to be a mirror for God.

He recognizes my growth.
He is full of trust for me.
He knows I will return his gentleness.
I will build up the light, life and love
in the image I carry of him.

He will soar in my heart.

As I grow
through ever cooler strata
from the earth's center outward,
as I fight glowing minerals,
vast underworld seas,
countless layers of slate,
bands of bedrock,
resistant skeletons of the past,

as I grow teeth,
fins, flippers, wings
and finally eyes,
I hope,
God,
that you will not lose me
in the innumerable faults of the earth
on my way up to the light,
and that you will have a warm blanket
of sheep's wool
ready for me
when I am done.

The craziness of lightning
rips into the steady growth
like some mindless shark
and throws you back
to the challenge of survival.

There is no time to flower.
There is only the frantic search of roots
to supply nourishment
to repair the deathwound.
There is the loss of needles
to concentrate energy
in one place,
to drive the life-force
into the shriek of that torn bark,
that open flesh.

There is only the bare eye
in its helpless flinching,
the wordless scream,
flung like a torn heart
into the cold air.

I experience the gentleness
of a filigree world,
of lace ribboned across the sky.

In deep care
this life expands.

The sun's warmth
is measured in fractions of degrees
and each bud knows its time
for bursting.

It is
as if silence
were the mother
and patience
the father
of growth.

God,
there are some paths
which I will not travel anymore.
Their comfort is death.
I will leave the safety
of their predictable markers.

I am a man with a commitment.
I carry my yearning
like a flower from you.
I am ready.
I try to move with your wind.
I am learning to let go.
I have chosen growth,
right through the pain
with its blindness and muzzle.

God,
treat me
like one
made in your image
and growing toward your likeness.
Help me
to believe in me
like you
believe in yourself.

She lives in three worlds:
the green world of growth,
her spring,
the yellow world of decline,
her autumn,
the dark world of death,
her winter.

She lives on all fronts,
challenges the colors,
makes them purer.
On good days she can see
that it has to be like this.
She knows that each gives meaning
to the other.

She knows
that each part of the cycle
is part of the circle
that has no beginning and end,
and that the plan is
to make an upward spiral
of that circle.

That in each dying we live
and in each living we die,
and in both we grow to completion,
to the perfect point of the spiral.

Like a stranger to myself
I take my arms
and put them around the inevitable.
Eye to eye
I choose to meet
what comes toward me.

There are passages in life
without angels.
Some nights are dark
and harbor angry dogs.
There are days without music,
they drone through my headaches
which spread out like a limitless plain.
I cannot laugh.
I do not have enough depth to cry.
Everything is a shallow gray.
I search out the colors
of a magical childhood.

But I know
that ultimately
I will grow through those alien moments.
And growing is keeping the vision,
not giving up,
experiencing the pain
here and now.

I always have a window left,
a window into visions,
into unimaginable blue,
into that rich nothing
at the edge of becoming.

On my journey through here
there is always the freedom
to refuse the mediocre,
to resist heartless repetition,
to oppose the habit of love,
to say no to all deathdealing.

And I will not give that window a name.
I will not narrow it down,
but just call it "my blue window"
and throw it open wide

in me.

All growth
leads to contact,
to touching
and being touched
where our life-force flows.

I don't have time
for the waiting rooms of small talk,
or to set empty gestures into the air,
to play at being alive,
to resolve religious problems.

My growing is
having a yearning that hurts,
being breakable by words alone,
and taking the risk
of living on the edge.

But that is how we meet.
Our brokenness touches
and in our craving for the light
we lift off,
dancing angels with weighty feet.

I want to grow into my skin,
that loose-fitting covering.
I want to grow into my hands,
those bony extensions.

I want to grow into my eyes,
those flexible lenses.
I want to grow into my words,
that assemblage of sounds.

I want to be at home
in me:

in my skin,
to experience the healing in contact;

in my hands,
that they guide gently in love;

in my iris and pupil,
to call into life
what is afraid of living;

in my words,
to unfold a story
that has a home for everyone.

I want to live in me.
I want to be where I am.
In being for me
I will be for you.

I try to follow
the strength of my yearning
and turn into a tree
with its profusion of branches and leaves
that fill the void
forever.

I grow wings
and lift off like an eagle
who needs no resting place.

I hug the earth
and turn into a blade of grass,
which is part of a rolling field
that knows no end.

I celebrate
the shape and shadow of life
from root to crown.
I inhabit my yearning
and create world upon world.

God is sometimes in a tree
that creates us.

Sometimes I wish to return
to the old, the warm, the known,
the way it was then.
Then I color that world with dreams,
I give it wings,
I make it bloom.
It glows.
I turn it into a bed
for my weary soul.
I ignore its portion of death
and retouch the shape of its heart.

But when I actually go there
the color recedes
and black tries to swallow me.
The wings turn to talons
already scratching my skin.
The blossoms are spots of blood.
That world swallows light.
The bed turns into a deathbed
and the repressed death
becomes an almighty shadow.
The retouched shape of the heart
is that of an infant.

I give in,
I know that all motion
is forward motion.
The rest is a fleeing.
And so I strike out once again,
the maze of possibilities
in front of me.

The blue of the ocean
with its eternal return,
its freedom to move in circles
around a patient world;

the blue of lupines,
a procession of signposts
through the wilderness;

the blue of your eyes
my love,
a world of adventure;

the unique shade of blue
of the blue jay, the blue crab,
the blue fox, the blue stone,
the blue whale and the bluebonnet,
each like a piece of heaven,
like a drop of water;

the blue of the mountain lake,
that single eye of God,
surrounded by its brother
the borderless green;

the graduated blue of mountain ridges
at advancing dusk,
beckoning ever homeward;

the blue of all shadows,
like light in reserve
waiting its turn to explode
in full brilliance.

I will take each as a reminder
to grow, grow and grow,
beyond each shade of blue
into that light
where all colors are shot through
and dissolved by His dazzling presence.

In my writing and photography I try to be essentially evocative. I do not try to prescribe but rather to evoke a response. I hope to touch a chord that gives rise to recognition. I do not know how the world should be, I don't have a yardstick by which to measure everything. Therefore my writing and photography are approximations. They are attempts to understand what is going on around and in me. I am searching. I write and photograph to create some kind of home for myself in this world, knowing all along that I will never be totally at home and also knowing that my time here is very limited. It is this sense of "home" that I wish to evoke in the reader/viewer.

To write and to photograph is to tap something that lies dormant, to search for a potential, for a new possibility. I have untilled soil in me, I am a learner and newcomer in the process of life, even though I have turned forty. I live amidst the mysteries of the life process and want to experience that process more consciously. And I want to respond to that process, and I wish for my responses to be fresh, alive, personal, rather than clichéd. To discover what lies dormant, to uncover what I did not know, is to be renewed, to live differently, to grow.

Sometimes I ask myself: Why write a line? Why take that picture? What is the point? And again and again I find that the answer has something to do with communication. To be human is to communicate, at least to try to communicate, to share, to let the other know where I am. I want to share what I am doing, because in sharing I break out of my isolation. I also can find out where others are in the life process, how they face similar situations, and I can hear and see their insights. I have found this sharing in its many forms to be very much at the center of my life, and I would be much poorer if I did not have it.

This is a book about growth. Growth in its many forms, in pain and joy, in reluctance and eagerness. In the past two years nothing has fascinated me as much as the question, What might it be to be truly mature? For that reason many of the texts came very naturally to me, though others needed more coaxing or pursuit. I want to challenge and be challenged, to grow beyond the mediocre, to leave stages behind me, to break new ground. In my photography I feel very attracted to growing things, particularly to trees, and could therefore express my feelings in images as well.

I look forward to new levels and insights and to experiencing things that I can't yet imagine.

ULRICH SCHAFFER
Burnaby, British Columbia, Canada

7 *Yucca, near Big Sur, California. I worked hard for this photo, crawling up a steep hill to shoot the plant against the blue Pacific.*

9 *Pine and moon, San Bernardino Mountains, California. Again and again I have been intrigued by the deep blue sky high in the California mountains. At times it looks almost unreal. For the blue skies of this book, I was careful generally to shoot with the sun at my back and my camera as much into the sky as possible, usually at about 90 degrees to the sun. Then I used a polarizing filter, which reduces the reflected light on everything. The polarizer does not change any colors but renders them more saturated.*

11 *Lupines, near my house in Burnaby, British Columbia. I spent several days trying to capture the magic of lupines. I chose this photograph because of its gentle quality. It is a double exposure. One of the images is exposed a shorter time, tending to make it disappear toward the back. The camera was moved slightly for the second exposure. In close-up work like this, it is necessary to look through the camera continuously until one has found a suitable subject. It is almost impossible to previsualize the photo. Moving the camera one centimeter can change the whole image totally.*

13 *Kelley Lake, Cariboo region of British Columbia. This is one of my favorite regions for fall photography, primarily because of the aspens in mid-October.*

15 *Maple and evergreens, near Seton Portage, British Columbia.*

17 *Oak, near Santa Maria, California.*

19 *Aspens in the San Francisco Mountains, Arizona. The white-on-white caught my eye.*

21 *Birch, near Squamish, British Columbia.*

23 *Catoneaster berries, Burnaby, British Columbia.*

25 *Fall forest near Hamburg, West Germany.*

27 *Rocks in Widgeon Creek, near Vancouver, British Columbia.*

29 *Aspens, San Francisco Mountains, Arizona. This is really a photo of the blue sky. The white trunks just show the blue sky more.*

31 *Fog in Stanley Park, Vancouver, British Columbia. In October and November the fog often just sits in the park in the mornings until it burns off. In the upper left a bit of blue sky is already visible. The sunlight gives the fog a luminescent quality. That is what I wanted to catch.*

33 *Reflections of skeletal trees, Nahatlatch Lakes, British Columbia.*

35 *Rocks, Point Lobos, near Carmel, California.*

37 *Beach with gulls, taken from a cliff, Oregon coast.*

39 *Dune with grasses, Oregon. This is perhaps the most demanding photo in the book, because there is so little on it. I shot it up a dune in a way that allowed me to get the sky in a straight line above the dune. It reminds me a little of some of the modern abstract painters who work with bold horizontal bands. I wanted that blue band to contrast with the very vulnerable grasses.*

41 Birch leaves near Squamish, British Columbia. To achieve the softness that I wanted in this picture, I set up the camera in such a way that one of the leaves almost touched the lens and was therefore very much out of focus. I was more interested in portraying an inner feeling than an outer landscape.

42 / 43 A field of rapeseed, north of Stuttgart, West Germany. Here it was the almost abstract design that interested me.

44 / 45 Pine branches reflected in a small puddle, near Long Beach, British Columbia. The brownish rocks in the right foreground seem like eggs in a bird's nest to me. The photo speaks to me of shelteredness.

46 / 47 Beech trees near Rotenburg/Wümme, West Germany. This is a double exposure. To a normal exposure I added another exposure totally out of focus. Through the out-of-focus image I hoped to be able to add a kind of halo effect to the trees to emphasize the light streaming through them.

49 Aspens in shadow, near Clinton, British Columbia.

51 Rock in pool, Garibaldi Lakes, near Vancouver, British Columbia. I wanted some surrealistic qualities in this photo. The rock seems to float on the water as well as in the clouds.

53 Boat, Island of Rhodes, Greece. By pointing the camera down and including much of the foreground, I wanted to give the photo more depth. The rocks lead the viewer into the photo. The same process then happens in the text.

55 Beech tree with hoar frost, Schauinsland, near Freiburg/Breisgau, West Germany. The Schauinsland (literally translated, "look into the land") is a ridge (part of the Black Forest) that is exposed to winds and weather. Because of that the trees have been "blown" into interesting shapes. The almost constant wind and the moisture in the air have formed this windblown design on the branches in this photo.

57 Reed, on the Oste River, West Germany. I had to crouch down and point my camera almost directly into the sun in order to get the silvery effect. A few rays of the sun were actually on the uncropped slide. The sky is underexposed to bring out the silver more. I had visualized the final result to be something like this but nevertheless was pleasantly surprised when I saw the photo. To me, surprise is a constant part of photography.

59 Aspens at sunset, near Clinton, British Columbia.

61 Tree and blue sky, Monument Valley, Arizona.

63 Driftwood and flowers, at the junction of the Taseko and Chilko rivers, British Columbia.

65 Dead tree, Botanie Valley, British Columbia.

67 Landscape with gentle lines, Island of Nordstrand, West Germany. I was intrigued by the simple lines of this landscape. The fog added a bit of mystery to the simplicity.

69 *Sunset near Goslar, West Germany. I was driving through the Harz Mountains when I noticed that the sunset might be beautiful. I had just enough time to pull into a small side road to look for an interesting foreground. The dead limbs of fallen trees seemed like threatening as well as primal forms. I picked up the primal idea in the text.*

71 *Tree struck by lightning, Botanie Valley, British Columbia.*

73 *Spring aspens, San Francisco Mountains, Arizona. This is a double exposure. For the second exposure I moved the camera slightly. By doing that I wanted to create a very soft-lined photo in pastel colors.*

75 *Beech forest, near Rotenburg/Wümme, West Germany.*

77 *Three-colored tree, near Lillooet, British Columbia.*

79 *Oak in lake, near Jolon, California.*

81 *Landscape north of Flagstaff, Arizona.*

83 *Two kites, at the annual kite festival in Vancouver, British Columbia.*

85 *Gunnera leaf, Burnaby, British Columbia. I chose to match the leaf with this poem because the leaf speaks to me of lifeblood, of energy in its veins.*

87 *Oak, east of Lodi, California. I was affected by two forms of a tree: one standing, the other having fallen over. It is almost as if it might be the same tree at different times.*

89 *Sunset over Oregon dunes.*

91 *Leaves in a puddle, Vancouver. I was intrigued by the dying leaves on the one hand and by the bright, lively blue on the other. Much of life seems to take place in that tension.*

Cover design by Karen Emerson
Text design by Design Office Bruce Kortebein
Text typography in Cartier by Turner & Brown, Inc.
Color separations and printing by Eastern Press
Text paper is 100# Mead Black and White Enamel Gloss
Flexibinding by A. Horowitz & Sons